Photo: Marcus Fülber

C-160 Transall

Transall C-160

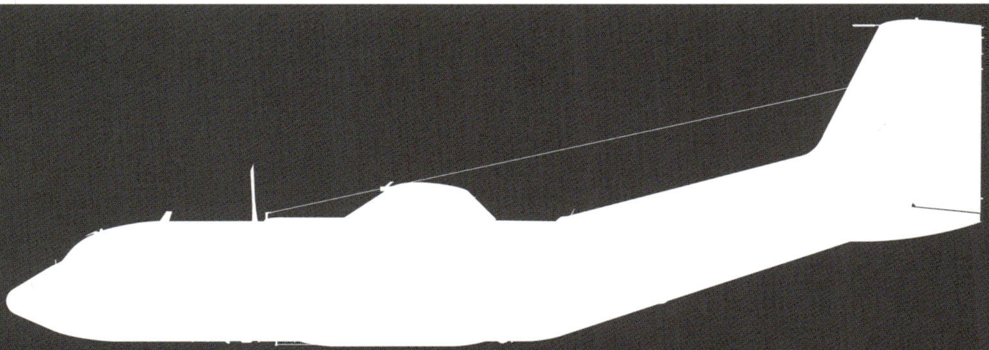

The C-160 Transall is one of those aircraft that is often taken for granted, but has had a very interesting history, all the while doing a pretty impressive job. When by the end of the 1950s both France and Germany were looking to replace their old Noratlas transport aircraft. The two countries considered to work together and design a completely new aircraft but the odds were against the project: the memory of the Second World War was still fresh in the minds and working with Germany on a military project might be considered rather sensitive. To make matters even more complicated, on the other side of the Atlantic, Lockheed had just presented the C-130 Hercules, an aircraft that could certainly do the job. However, in an effort to promote the French and German aviation industries, the project went ahead after some heavy lobbying. The result was to become the C-160 Transall - with the "C" of cargo, the "160" describing the wingsurface of 160 m² and "Transall" coming from the project's name "Transporter Allianz".

Today, with the A400M Atlas slowly but surely replacing the Transall, the days of the elegant transport aircraft are counted, its career already spanning an impressive 54 years. In all, 214 Transalls have been built and many of them have seen every corner of the world. Not that many books have been written on the aircraft, so we really wanted to do a good job presenting it. This was only possible with the extensive help from two gentlemen who also have a soft spot for the aircraft: Jens Schymura and Marcus Fülber. Together with the photos from some of our other regular photographers, we got to this result. I hope you like it!

Photo: Marcus Fülber

Special thanks to: Marcus Fülber, Jens Schymura, Andreas Zeitler, Stephan Ortmann, Laurent Heyligen, Peter Anthoni, Kris Christiaens and as always Gunter Geens.

Photo: Marcus Fülber

Above: A Luftwaffe Transall touches down after a transport mission. This aircraft looks pretty clean, but some, as you will discover in this book, can get pretty dirty and shaded! Look at the deployed speed brakes on top and underneath the wings. The C-160 Transall made it's first flight in February of 1963, but it wouldn't enter service until 1967. Initially, Germany ordered 110 aircraft, while France placed an order for 50 of them. Later, in 1977, the latter ordered 25 more.

Photo: Marcus Fülber

Transall variants

The 214 aircraft that were built were operated by 4 different countries: Germany, that ordered 110 of them, France, that ordered 75, Turkey, that bought 20 of the type and finally South Africa, that operated 9, but retired them more than 20 years ago. The aircraft that were used in Germany were designated C-160D. Some of these aircraft were fitted with a self-protection suite, called ESS, to be recognised by the Warning Systems fixed to the fuselage.

The initial aircraft delivered to the French Armée de l'Air received the designation C-160F. A second batch of aircraft was ordered, with the first delivered in 1981. These aircraft were the C-160 NG - Nouvelle Generation, or New Generation. They no longer had the large lateral cargo door on the port side of the fuselage and introduced an in-flight refuelling probe and an additional fuel tank in the center section of the wing. Some of the initial C-160Fs were upgraded to the NG standard and hence became the C-160R - R standing for "Renové" or "upgraded".

Photo: Marcus Fülber

Photo: Armée de l'Air et de l'Espace

Left: This photo shows the two sole existing C-160G Gabriel, a version of the Transall, developped for electronic reconnaissance, easily to distinguish by the antennas fitted to the aircraft and the radome on the lower fuselage that can be lowered in flight. Notice also the different wing tips and the in-flight refuelling probe. On the aft fuselage, more electronics are located underneath a teardrop dome.
The C-160G aircraft are based on the C-160 NG and stationned at the air base of Evreux, to the west of Paris.

The 20 Turkish C-160s were bought from the Luftwaffe in 1971 and received the designation C-160T. The South African aircraft were known as the C-160Z.

Photo: Marcus Fülber

Photo: Marcus Fülber

Time to get a closer look at the details of the aircraft and traditionally, we begin with the nose. The black radome houses a weather radar and hinges upwards for easy access. These photos show Transalls of LTG - Lufttransportgeschwader - 63, based at Hohn Air Base in Schleswig-Holstein in northern Germany. The photo above shows how the wing is basically placed on top of the aircraft, ensuring optimal room in the cargo bay. Notice the windscreen wipers in front of the pilot- and co-pilots station.

Right: The crew entrance door is located on the port side of the forward fuselage. On either side of the nose, an easy access panel is located, giving access to the battery compartment.

Below right: The nose landing gear of this German Transall is completely compressed - see how close the aircraft sits to the ground?

Below: On top of the fuselage, pitot tubes are located; a double one on the port side, a single on the starboard side.

Photo: Marcus Fülber

Photo: Marcus Fülber

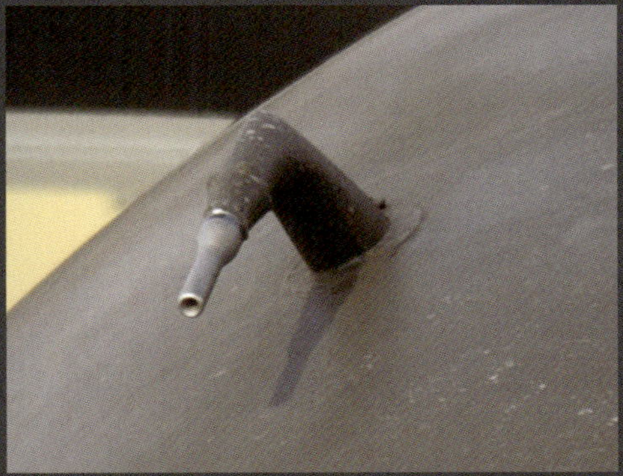

Photo: Marcus Fülber

Photo: Marcus Fülber

Photo: Jens Schymura

Above: The starboard side of the forward fuselage with the cockpit side windows. Notice the patchwork paintjob and the pitot-tube covers.

Photo: Marcus Fülber

Above: A close-up of the foward cockpit windows. In front of the central window, an airscoop can be seen that is typical for the German aircraft. Notice the windscreen wipers.

Photo: Marcus Fülber

Left: This photo shows the modifications of the ESS self defence suite that some of the German Transalls received. Most prominent is the sensor that warns the crew whenever a missile is launched at the aircraft. Behind it is a search light.

Opposite page: This spectacular head-on view is of a French C-160G Gabriel, the electronic reconnaissance version of the Transall. It is based on the C-160NG and thus equipped with an in-flight refuelling probe and can easily be recognised by the many antennas attached to it.

Transall C-160
Forward Fuselage

Photo: Malaury Buis, Armée de l'Air et de l'Espace

Photo: Marcus Fülber

The photo above shows the set-up of the Transall to good effect: a transport aircraft with a very low placed fuselage, granting easy access for cargo and troops, a high placed wing offering lots of space for the large engine propellers and large horizontal and vertical tails for optimal manoeuvrability. The Transall is equipped with two engines, giving the aircraft a top speed of just over 500 km/h and a range of about 1,800 km. The Transall is smaller than the 4-engined Lockheed C-130 Hercules, even though the wingspan of both aircraft is almost the same: 40 meter for the Transall, 40,41 meter for the C-130.

Right: A close-up of the crew entrance door, indicating that only 1 person should stand on it at the time.

Photo: Jens Schymura

Transcall C-160 Forward Fuselage

These photos show the crew entrance door, located on the port side of the forward fuselage. It is fixed to the fuselage by means of two hinges and lowered by extending a pair of actuators. Next to the door is the ground earth static connection. The cockpit can be accessed by mounting 5 more steps, very much like in the C-130 - see book DH-009.

Photo: Jens Schymura

Photo: Jens Schymura

Photo: Jens Schymura

Photo: Andreas Zeitler

Above: This Luftwaffe Transall is firing flares from the dispencers bolted on top of the fuselage and the pods underneath the wings. Only German aircraft are equipped with these.

Right: An updated C-160R of the Armée de l'Air. There are quite few new features to be found on the forward fuselage. First is the omission of the large lateral cargo door on the port side of the fuselage. On top of the fuselage, an in-flight refuelling probe can be seen. The French Transalls are the only ones that are equipped with this probe. Immediately aft of the radome, next to the nose gear bay, Radar Warning Receivers are located. Also notice the different type of blade antennas on the wings and fuselage.

Photo: Andreas Zeitler

Transall C-160 Forward Fuselage

Photo: Jens Schymura

Above: A ground crew member is about to insert new sets of flares in the dispencers located on top of the fuselage of the Transall of LTG61, based at Landsberg-Lech Air Base in the southern Germany, not far from München. Notice the round white GPS antenna on top of the fuselage.

Photo: Jens Schymura

Right: When flying in hostile environments, the Transall needs to be equipped with self-protecting equipment, such as flares and chaff, which reduce the danger of being shot down by shoulder carried heat-seeking missiles. For this, the Transall can be equipped with dispencers fixed to the top of the forward fuselage or pods that are carried underneath the wings. More details of the latter can be found on pages 98 and 99.

Photo: Marcus Fülber

Transall C-160
Fuselage

German Transalls have, during their 54 year long career, often been adorned with a special livery. To be honest, some of them were rather flashy, but this "Retro Brummel" for me is one of the most beautiful ever done. The aircraft of LTG63, based in Hohn air base was presented in 2021 and went on a Goodbye Tour, marking the end of service for the type within the Luftwaffe. The top of the wings sport a giant German and French flag with in the middle the map of the world, indication the theatre of operations for the type. A giant bumblebee - possibly one of the best words in English - is painted on the port side of the fuselage, indicating the unit's logo. From the end of 2021 on, the Luftwaffe's only transport aircraft is the Airbus A400M Atlas. Hopefully its career can be as long as the Transall's.

Below: On the port side of the forward fuselage of the C-160D and C-160F, a lateral cargo door is located, which can be opened upward by means of two actuators near the top of it. When the Armée de l'Air ordered 25 additional Transalls in teh early 1980s, this lateral door was omitted.

Photo: Jens Schymura

Photo: Marcus Fülber

Photo: Andreas Zeitler

Above: 2016 marked the 60th anniversary of the Luftwaffe in its current form and for this occasion, C-160D 50 + 95 got this very distinctive livery, depicting a timeline on the fuselage and important moments for the unit. Notice 1 million flying hours on the Transall in 2011.

Left: A particularly clean French Transall NG - New Generation. This and the Transall R - Rénové, or modernised - have been updated on several parts. One of the most obvious modifications is the installation of an in-flight refuelling probe.

Photo: Marcus Fülber

Above: A pair of French C-160 Rs are about to start their engines for another mission. Notice the position and angle of the in-flight refuelling probe, which is slightly canted upwards. Look at the dayglo markings on the aft part of the fuselage, indicating the tanker capability of the aircraft.

Photo: Jens Schymura

Above: On either side of the fuselage, an armoured plate is attached close to where the propeller blades are located. In case of engine trouble or an engine exploding this plate will prevent the fast moving propeller blades to cut the aircraft into pieces.

Right: Another special livery for an aircraft of LTG63. Next to the large squadron emblem, the EATC logo can be seen - European Air Transport Command, a collaboration grouping transport wings of several European countries, with headquarters in Eindhoven, The Netherlands. Notice the feathered propeller blades.

Photo: Jens Schymura

Photo: Marcus Fülber

Left: A C-160D Transall assigned to LTG63 is about to land on the Hohn airbase runway. Notice the size of the vertical tail with the extended base as well as the 4-bladed propellers. These reversible-pitch, constant-speed BAe 4/8000/6 propellers are built by Ratier Figeac in France.

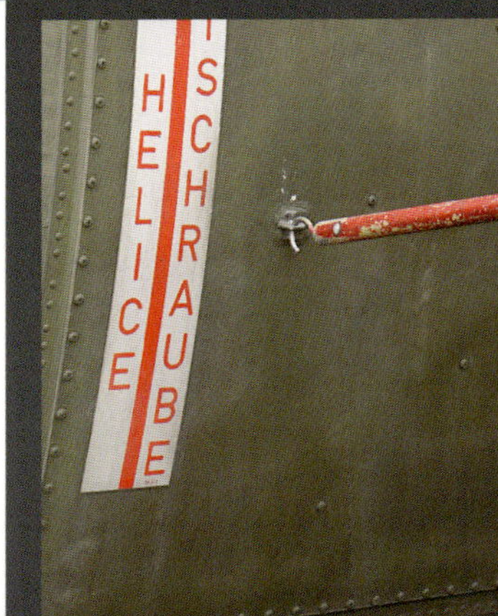

Photo: Jens Schymura

Right: When parked, the propeller blades of the Transall can be placed in a fixed position by means of a bar that is connected to the fuselage. This photo shows the port landing gear sponson, which also houses the aircraft's APU - Auxiliary Power Unit - which provides the aircraft with electrical power. The round panel with the large 'E" over it, is the ground electrical power attachment point. The photo above it shows the connection of the holding bar to the fuselage.

Photo: Jens Schymura

Photo: Marcus Fülber

Photo: Jens Schymura

Above: In 2011, LTG63 celebrated its 50th anniversary by means of this special dark grey painted C-160D, covered with stars and silhouettes of the aircraft flown by the unit over the years. You can spot the Transall on the tail, in front of the outlines of Schleswig-Holstein, the northernmost province of Germany, where the unit is located. More to the front, renders of a Dornier Do-28, Bell UH-1D and a Nordatlas can be seen. The emblems on the tail represent the Alt Duvenstedt, Hugo Junkers-Kaserne and Hohn Fliegerhorst.

Left: A close-up of the starboard fuselage with the landing gear sponson, which houses the refuelling point.

Photo: Marcus Fülber

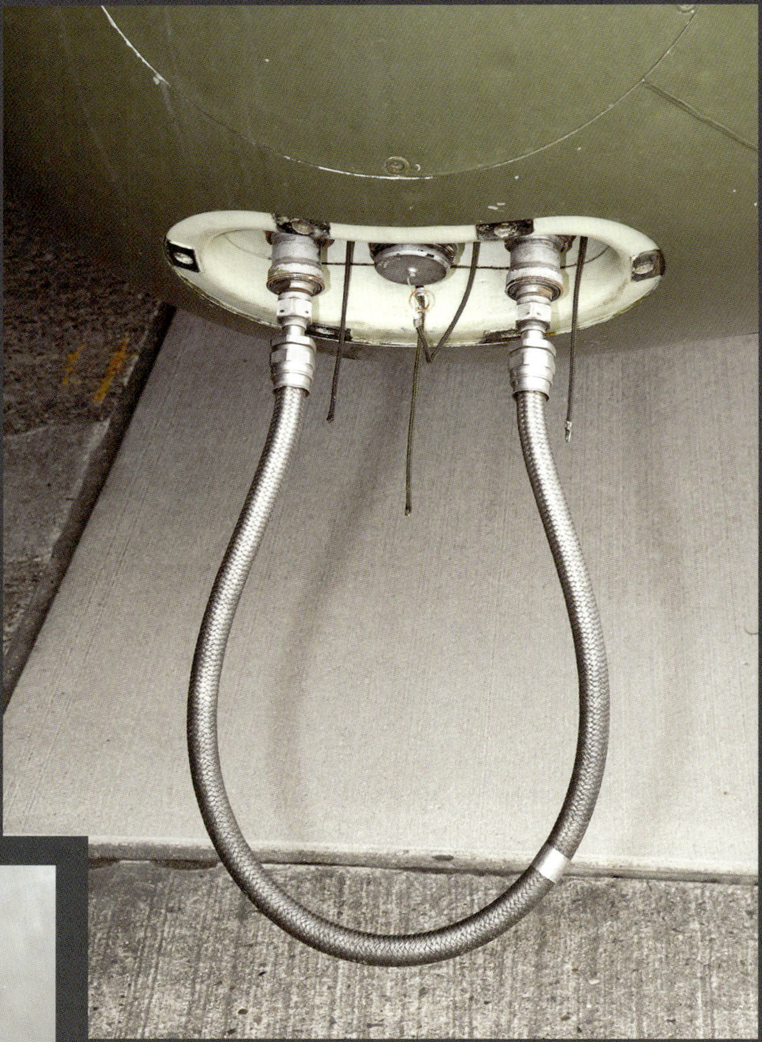

Photo: Marcus Fülber

Photo: Jens Schymura

The photos on these pages show some of the details of the port landing gear sponson of the Transall. It not only houses the sturdy landing gear, but also other important parts of the aircraft, such as the APU- Auxiliary Power Unit. The connections in the photo above, fixed to the front of the port sponson, are for filling, draining and testing of the hydraulic system, with the main circuit 1 - green - and the auxiliary circuit 1 - red.

Left and above left: At the front of the port main gear sponson, the ground power hook is located. The black and yellow indication is for the Fire Extinguishing System for the Auxiliary Power Unit.

Photo: Jens Schymura

Above: The mid-section of the fuselage on the port side. Looking at the sand and dust sitting on the aircraft, it could well have been to Afghanistan and back ... The panel on the aft part of the sponson can be filled with flares and chaff

Photo: Jens Schymura

Right: This is the hot air exhaust of the Auxiliary Power Unit, situated in the front part of the sponson. In the maintenance section of this book, we show you the APU in detail and out of the aircraft. The system is designed to deliver compressed air for main engine starting, but also air conditioning and the heating systems of the aircraft. The quick-release panel situated above it gives access to the fuel drainage point. All stencelling on the aircraft is indicated in both French and German, so Attention! and Achtung!

Photo: Andreas Zeitler

Left: A pair of French Transalls await their next mission. Look how far forward the in-flight refuelling probe extends. Immediately behind the radome, missile warning receivers are located on either side of the fuselage. On the starboard side of the fuselage, an emergency exit is located, seen in detail in the photo below. This exit can also be opened from the outside, by pulling the ring, turning the handle and pushing the door inwards.

Photo: Peter Anthoni

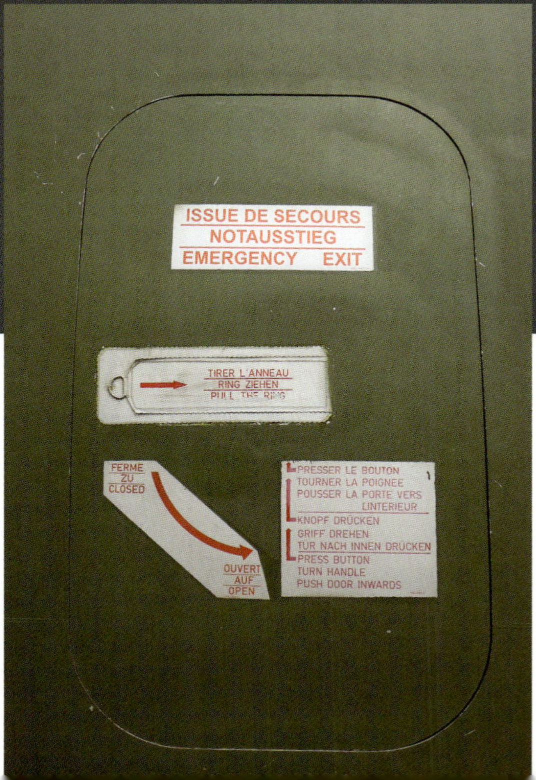

Photo: Marcus Fülber

Photo: Andreas Zeitler

Right: This unmarked Transall is the sole surviving C-160Z of the South African Air Force, seen at the South African Air Force Museum at Swartop Air Base near Pretoria in 2008. The country operated 9 of the type from 1970 on and started to face them out in 1996. All of them but this one were scrapped.

Photo: Marcus Fülber

Photo: Jens Schymura

Right: On either side of the aft fuselage, immediately aft of the main landing gear sponsons, troop cargo doors are located, through which up to 70 fully equipped paratroopers can be parachuted. These doors open first inwards and then slide upwards into the cargo bay. Just forward of the door is an area that in case of an emergency can be cut open, whenever the door is jammed.

Below: A Transall is taking off from Hohn airbase in northern Germany. The aircraft proved to be quite agile, which is an asset when flying into or from hostile places. On Youtube you can find some videos of Transalls performing a roll, although that probably isn't with any cargo or paratroopers in the back...

Photo: Jens Schymura

Photo: Jens Schymura

Above: A nicely weathered C-160 is taxiing back to its parking spot and gives us a good view of the aircraft's profile and slightly nose-down postion. 50 + 74 is carrying chaff/flare pods underneath the wing tips. Look how streamlined the engines are. The propellers of the Transall turn anti-clockwise, when seen from behind the aircraft.

Photo: Marcus Fülber

Right: The aft fuselage seen from the starboard side. Look at all the rivets that run over it. Also noticable is the opening between the fuselage and the aft part of the wing centre section. In this photo, the wing's trailing edge flaps are completely down and the troop cargo door is open. By the looks of it, this aircraft has recently been in maintenance and freshly repainted!

Photo: Laurent Heyligen

Photo: Jens Schymura

Photo: Jens Schymura

More photos of the aft fuselage of the Transall. The top photo shows one of the 20 aircraft that the Turkish Air Force purchased from the Luftwaffe in 1971 and received the designation C-160T. Notice that the radome has the same colour as the fuselage and that the propeller tips are painted in national red and white.

Photo: Marcus Fülber

Some more close-ups of the structure of the aft fuselage of the Transall. Look at all those rivets! The photo to the left shows the aft fuselage on the starboard side of the special painted Retro Brummel, which was presented in early 2021. Look at the artistic rendering of a Transall shooting flares!

Below: The same area, but this time on the port side of the fuselage. Look at the different structures of the base of the vertical tail and the many different shades of the camouflage due to maintenance, dirt and exhaust.

Photo: Jens Schymura

Photo: Andreas Zeitler

Above: A great overall view of a Transall of the Armée de l'Air, sitting very low on the tarmac. Look at the shape of the propeller blades and the opened intake on the port main landing gear sponson for the APU. Typical for the French Transall R, NG and G is the in-flight refuelling probe on top of the fuselage and the Radar Warning Receivers underneath the nose, immediately aft of the radome and on top of the fuselage. Notice that this version of the Transall doesn't have the lateral cargo door. The French C-160NG has an improved range over the initial C-160F, thanks to the addition of a fifth fuel tank, which is located in the centre section of the wing, on top of the cargo bay. Between 1994 and 1999, the French aircraft were modernised with updated digital systems, Head-Up Displays - HUD - and GPS navigation systems.

Photo: Andreas Zeitler

Photo: Peter A.nthoni

Above: Have a closer look at this dynamic photo of an updated Transall of the Armée de l'Air and see if you can spot all the differences with the standard Transall. Notice that this version doesn't have the large lateral cargo door but in stead is equipped with an in-flight refuelling pod. On the nose, aft of the radome, a Radar Warning receiver can be seen - another one is located on the starboard side - and above the main gear sponson, a fuselage pod is located. On top of the fuselage, in front of the wing, a pair of airscoops are positionned.

Photo: Peter A.nthoni

Right: This photo is of the same aircraft as above and shows the fuselage pod immediately in front of the side cargo door. Look at all the spots of different grey paint all over the fuselage and wings. The insides of the main gear doors of the French Transalls are painted chrome green.

The Transall's long wings

The C-160 Transall thanks much of its agility to the long wings mounted on top of the fuselage. The Transall has a wingspan of exactly 40 meter and is equipped with trailing edge flaps that can be lowered in two parts, as seen in these photos. Each wing has three flaps, with smaller inboard ones and wider outboard ones, running all the way to the ailerons. The photo below shows the structure of the port wing - notice how the inboard flap is stained by the engine exhaust. At the top of the photo, the lower speed brakes are deployed and the internal structure is visible.

Photo: Jens Schymura

Photo: Stephan Ortmann

Below: The port engine and the brown-metal coloured exhaust. Stains and heat from the engines runs as far back as the horizontal tails. The leading edge of the wings is painted black.

Photo: Stephan Ortmann

An Armée de l'Air C-160G Gabriel patrols over the Atlantic coast. Look at the span of this aircraft! Notice the many antennas all around the aircraft and the wingtip pods, typical for this version of the Transall and the in-flight refuelling probe. Look how the engine exhausts stain the horizontal tails. The C-160Gs are based at Evreux in north-western France.

Photo: Malaury Buis, Armée de l'Air et de l'Espace

Photo: Marcus Füllber

Above: The 2021 Retro Brummel - Bumblebee - is flying over the coastal area, not far from the Danish border. On top of the wings, written over the French and German flags, "Last Call" indicates that the end is near for the loyal workhorse. By the end of 2021, the type was replaced with the much larger and faster Airbus A400M Atlas. Notice the walkway lines on top of the fuselage, wings and horizontal tails in this photo.

Right: A close-up of the starboard wing, seen from below, with the flap actuators and push mechanisms. The flaps are lowered during landing, take off and low speed manoeuvres.

Photo: Jens Schymura

Photo: Jens Schymura

Photo: Jens Schymura

Below: Moments after getting airborne, this French Transall is banking to the left, giving us a good view of the upper wing surface. Notice the trailing edge flaps and the spoilers on top of the wing. Having been in use for several decades, the camouflage of the Transall often start to look like patchwork.

Photo: Laurent Heyligen

Photo: Jens Schymura

Photo: Stephan Ortmann

Photo: Jens Schymura

Top: Transall 50 + 17 is taking off, while a visiting Austrian Eurofighter Typhoon is being towed in the background.
Above: The port wingtip seen from below, with antennas fixed to the leading edge and a navigation light at the very end of it. The photo to the right shows the extended speed brakes on top of the port wing.

Photo: Jens Schymura

Above: The Transall is equipped with perforated speed brakes that are located on top and underneath the wings. In all, there are 8 of them. This photo shows the two on top of the starboard wing - the inboard ones are small, the outboard ones about double the length. They are equipped with 2 and 3 actuators respectively.

Photo: Jens Schymura

Above: Close-up of the lower speed brakes on the starboard wing. Notice the small red dots, absorbing the shock of the rectracting brakes.

Photo: Jens Schymura

Photo: Jens Schymura

Left and above: The speed brakes seen from the front and the back. Look at the position of the trailing edge flap actuators in between and next to the brakes.

Photo: Jens Schymura

Photo: Stephan Ortmann

Photo: Jens Schymura

Top: The span of the trailing edge flaps is apparent in this photo of a Transall taxiing toward its parking spot.

Above and right: details of the flap actuators and actuator housing.

Photo: Jens Schymura

Photo: Jens Schymura

Above left: The starboard wing tip of a German Transall, with the black blade antenna and the navigation light.

Left and below: The engine of the aircraft and the many inlets, drainages and exhausts all over it. Each engine has 4 large acces doors which can be easily opened by means of push buttons.

Photo: Jens Schymura

Photo: Jens Schymura

63
CALL

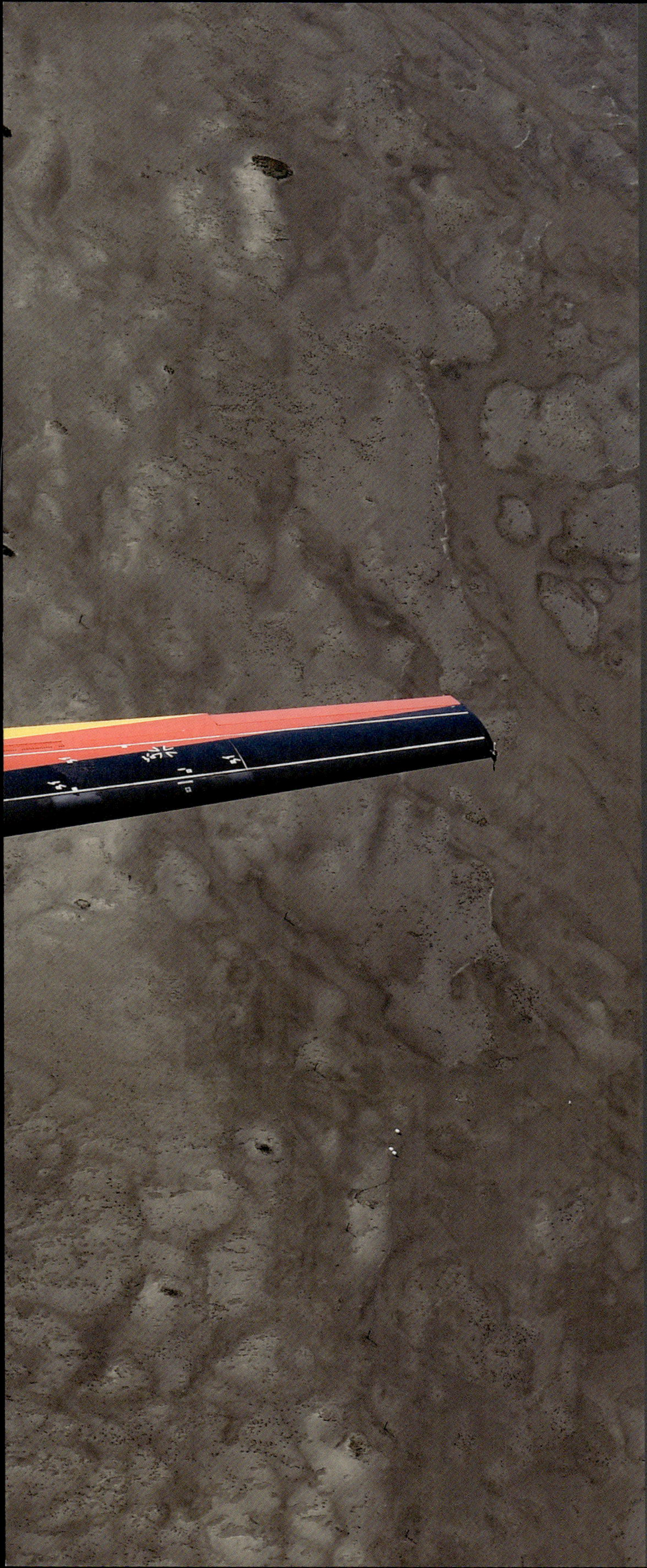

C-160 Transall
Wings

The design team of the Transall opted for a solution with 2 rather than 4 engines, which meant that the aircraft would be cheaper to fly and maintain, compared to its contemporary collegue, the C-130 Hercules. This partly compensated the higher purchase price of the Transall. The aircraft is powered by two Rolls-Royce RTy.20 Tyne Mk 22 turboprop engines, delivering some 6,100 HP each.

Below: The forward panels of the starboard engine are opened, granting technician access to the Rolls-Royce Tyne engine. Notice how the lower engine panel is fixed to the side one.

Photo: Peter Anthoni

Photo: Jens Schymura

Above: A close-up of the starboard engine spinner. The propellers are fully feathering constant-speed reversible-pitch ones and have a diameter of just over 5,48 meter.

Above: The port engine spinner and propeller base. The black painted front part is fixed to the engine itself, while the other parts can be opened quickly for inspection of the vital parts of the engine.

Above: Immediately below of the spinner, the engine's air intake is located. The Tyne engine - named after a river in England - was developpped for the Vickers Vanguard, but was mostly used in the Transall and the Breguet Atlantic maritime patrol aircraft.

Photo: Jens Schymura

Right: The Rolls-Royce RTy.20 Tyne engine is located forward of the wings leading edge which gives maintenance crew an unobstructed access. The engine itself is 2,76 meter long and comes in at a dry weight of 1,085 kg. This Luftwaffe Transall is equipped with a flare/chaff pod fixed to an under-wing pylon.

Photo: Jens Schymura

Above: The engine exhaust of the starboard engine. The exhaust is pointed downwards, mid wing. Notice how the aft part of the engine cover extends toward the flaps.

Photo: Jens Schymura

Above: Immediately aft of the engine exhaust, a drainage pipe is located. The Rolls-Royce engine is rather compact for such a large engine and has a diameter of 1,4 meter.

Transall C-160 Gabriel

The Armée de l'Air operates two Transalls that were modified from the NG-standard to a SIGNIT role - Signal Intelligence - and are used as surveillance platforms. These aircraft received the designation C-160G and are referred to as "Gabriel". During the first Gulf War, these aircraft saw extensive action. The Gabriel is a completely passive aircraft, capable of detecting, identify and locate enemy radars, but not to jam them. The cargo bay of the aircraft is modified to give room to about a dozen operators for the electronic equipment.

The photo to the right shows a huge amount of interesting details of the C-160G. Most prominent 5 huge antenna blades on top of the fuselage and the in-flight refuelling probe. Look how far aft the probe housing actually runs. Aft of it, at the base of the wings, two air intakes are located. The windows on the side of the fuselage are covered and armour plating is fixed to either side of the forward fuselage. Underneath the fuselage, the radar dome has been lowered; notice also the large yellow blade antennas next to the forward landing gear bay. Specific to the Gabriel are the blade antennas underneath the main gear sponsons.

Photo: Jean-Luc Brunet, Armée de l'Air et de l'Espace

C-160 Transall
C-160G

Photo: Malaury Buis - Armée de l'Air et de l'Espace

Photo: Andreas Zeitler

Photo: Laurent Heyligen

Photo: Laurent Heyligen

Top: One of the Gabriels is taking off for another mission. On the fuselage, aft of the troop cargo door, electronic equipment is placed in a teardrop radome. Also notice the bulge at the vertical tail's extended base.

Above: The wingtip of the C-160G carries an electronics pod with different style antennas attached to it.

Photo: Jean-Luc Brunet, Armée de l'Air et de l'Espace

Above: The two operational C-160G have code GS of GT, placed on the aft fuselage. This aircraft has the ventral radome lowered. Notice how the windows of the cargo bay have been covered, except for the ones of the troop door.
Right: Because of the equipment stored in the cargo bay, the C-160G is about 6 tons heavier than the standard Transall. This is why the in-flight refuelling probe isn't a luxury for the Gabriel.

Photo: Jens Schymura

The Transall's Cockpit

Time to take the 5 steps towards the cockpit of the Transall. For this, Jens Schymura and Marcus Fülber visited LTG63 at Hohn Airbase, where their contacts were generous in showing what flying the Transall is all about. As you can see in these photos, the cockpit of the aircraft is very hands-on, especially when you compare it to "luxury" cockpit such as those of the A400M Atlas, the aircraft replacing the Transall. Initially, the Transall had a crew of 5, with a pilot in the left seat and the co-pilot in the right seat. In between, aft of the central console, the flight engineer is seated. Aft of them, was the navigators' station, but with modern navigation systems, this post is no longer necessary. The final crew member is the load master.

Photo: Jens Schymura

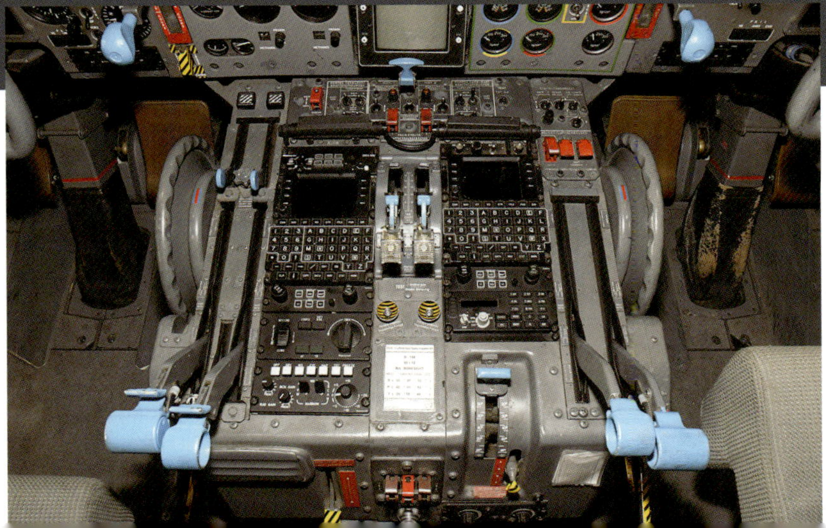

Photo: Marcus Fülber

Above: Although the clocks in the middle of the control columns have been removed, this is the cockpit of an operational Transall. The half-steering wheel to the left of the pilot's seat is to operate the nosewheel and manoeuvre the aircraft on the ground. The central instrument console holds the aircraft's throttles, one set for the pilot and another for the co-pilot. Immediately in front of the throttle is the Safety Lever and forward of that, the small blue Idle Levers. In the middle, also in light blue, are the two Condition Levers. The throttles are fully forward during take off and back at 62 degrees during ground idle. When pulled back to 70 degrees, the aircraft is in "Reverse".

Photo: Marcus Fülber

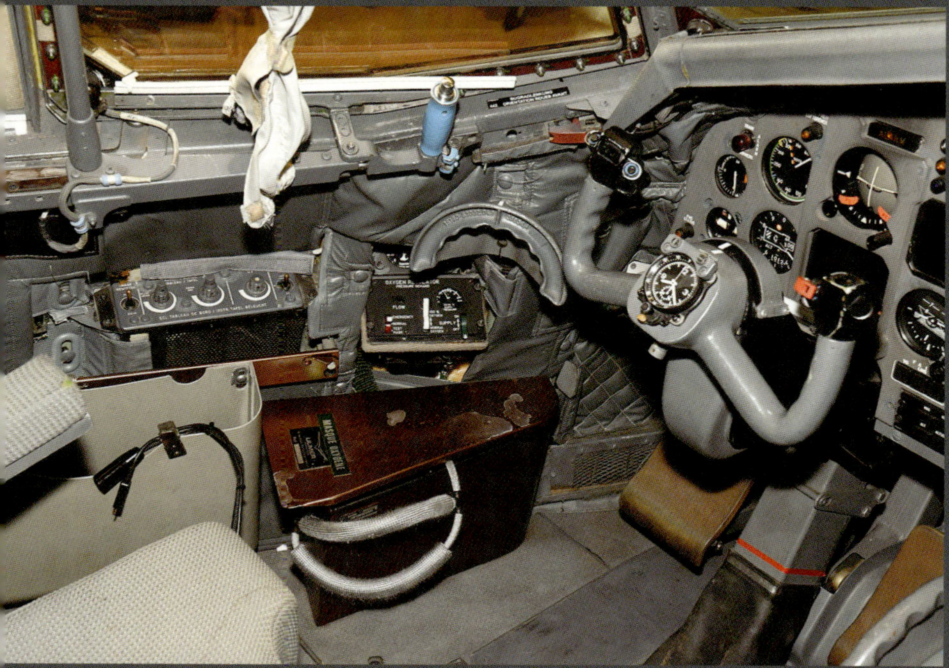

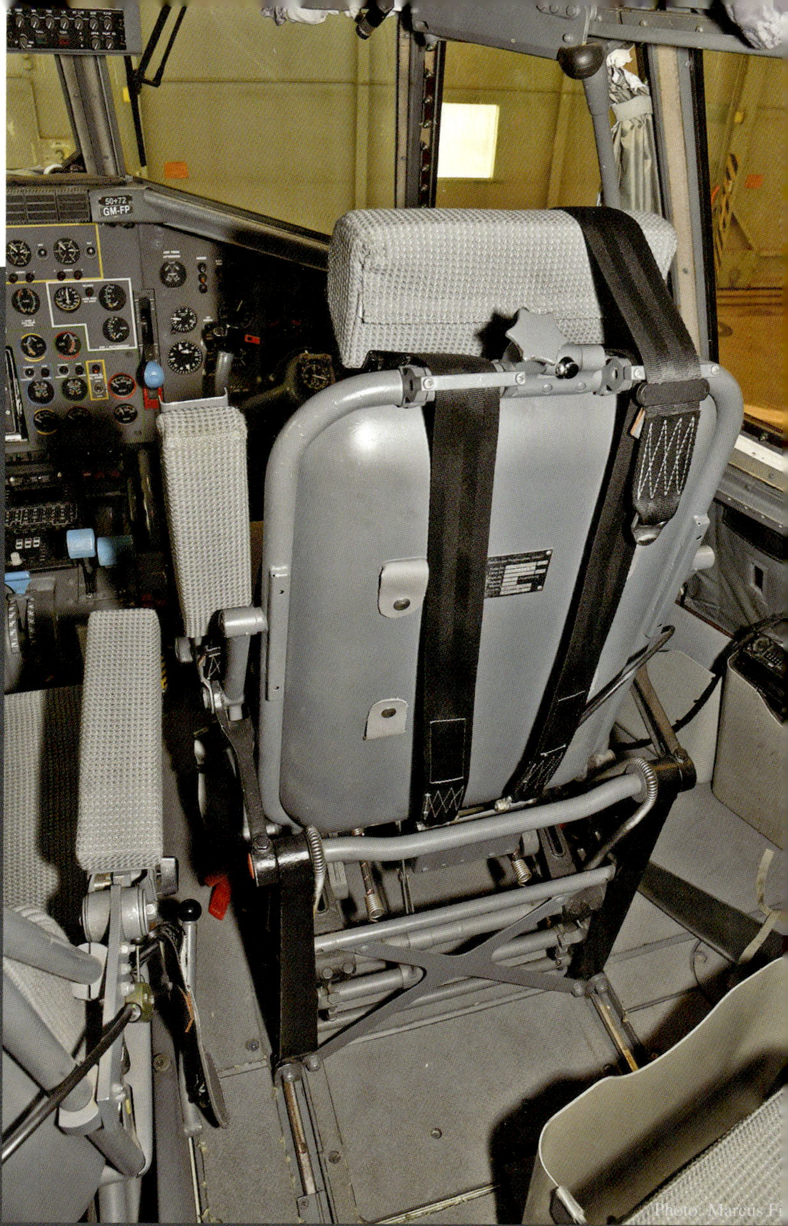

Photo: Marcus Fülber

Above: This is what is on the left side of the pilot, with the steering wheel for the nose wheel next to the control column. below it is a dark brown case containing the oxygen mask for the pilot, with the regulator panel next to it.
Below: This is what the co-pilot sees to his right; he too has an oxygen mask case and regulator. above it are controls for the instrument lights.

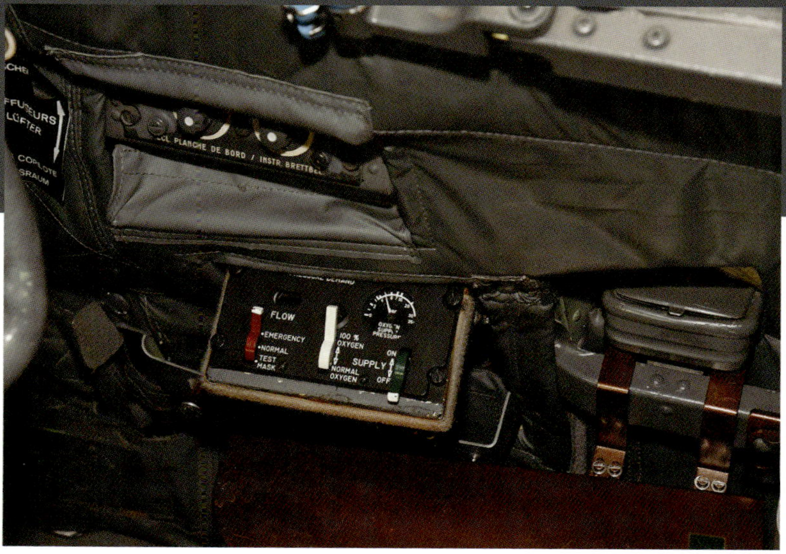

Photo: Marcus Fülber

Photo: Marcus Fülber

Right: This photo shows the overhead instrument panel. the four large levers on either side of it with the black round bases are the fuel valves. In this photo their are in the closed postion - Fermé, zu. Near the end of the panel, are the switches for the Electrical Power Supply. The panel holds switches and indicators for many of the aircraft's functions, from pressurisation, lights, cabin heat or engine fire extinguishers and air conditionning. Immediately above the pilot is the yellow and black crash bar.

Photo: Jens Schymura

Photo: Jens Schymura

Photo: Jens Schymura

Photo: Andreas Zeitler

In this photo, the crew of a Transall is flying over the runway of its home base. Remember the fuel valve levers next to the overhead instrument console? In this photo they are pushed forward - obviously. Although the crew have a good all-around view, sometimes blocking out the sun can be handy. On top of the main instrument panel is the failure warning panel, indicating fire or overheating of the engines. The large blue lever on the instrument panel indicates that the landing gear is still up, so no tactical landing on this approach. This is also called the Sarajevo Approach, during which the aircraft is flown towards the runway at a very steep angle, only to be pulled horizontally very close to the ground. A pretty impressive sight from both the cockpit and on the ground.

Photo: Marcus Fülber

Left: a look at the pilot and co-pilot seat, which can be adjusted to everyone's needs. The entire cockpit is padded. The photo above gives another close-up of the overhead instrument panel. Now where is that magnifying glass... Below: Aft of the central instrument console, the Oxygen Regulator and Emergency Brake handle are located.

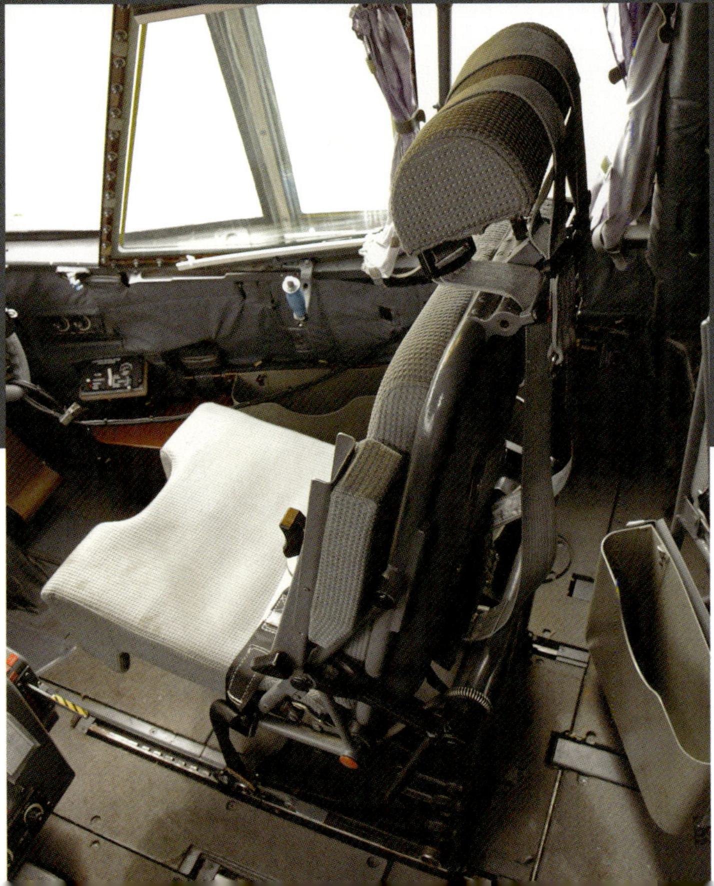

Photo: Marcus Fülber

Photo: Marcus Fülber

Behind the co-pilot's seat, the navigator's position is located. During the day, a small porthole helps him to see what he's doing, during the night, an overhead light does the trick. The seat can swivel 360 degrees. Because the navigational equipment has improved over the course of the Transall's service life, there is no longer need for a navigator. Not surprisingly, this means the seat is usually facing forward. Notice a document case to the side of it.

Below right: An emergency exit hatch can be found in the cockpit ceiling.

Photo: Jens Schymura

Photo: Jens Schymura

Photo: Jens Schymura

Photo: Jens Schymura

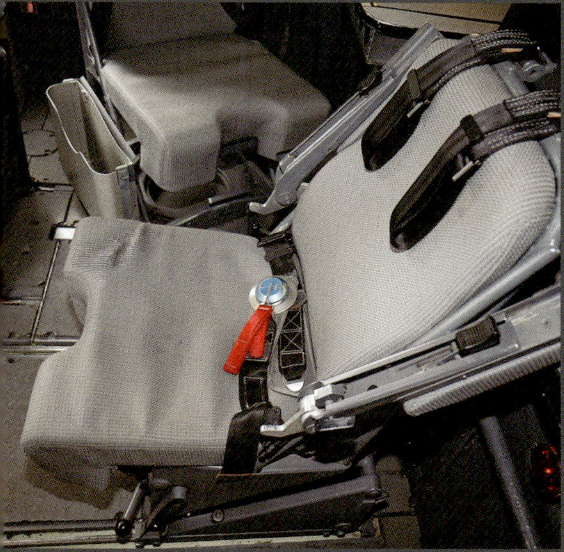

Above: The flight engineer's seat, located immediately aft of the central instrument console. This seat doesn't have a head rest like the seats of the pilot and co-pilot.

Photo: Jens Schymura

Above: A closer look at the instruments located at the navigators position. Comfy little table in front of it and a series of circuit breakers above it. Can you spot the aircraft's registration? It's 50 + 72.

Photo: Jens Schymura

Above: Next to the navigator's post, a bench is located with over it another series of circuit breakers. In front of it is the escape hatch in the ceiling of the cockpit.

Photo: Jens Schymura

Photo: Peter Anthoni

Landing the Transall

The C-160 Transall is designed to operate from small runways anywhere in the world or even unpaved runways. The photo above illustrates just how versatile the aircraft actually is, by landing on a beach! The Transall is designed to land at a distance of just 360 meter at normal landing weights and take off again almost fully loaded in a mere 1,100 meter.

Photo: Stephan Ortmann

Right: The landing gear of the Transall consists of two main gears with each 4 wheels and a nose gear with 2 wheels. Look how low the aircraft sits on the landing gear, making sure that cargo can easily be loaded into the bay. The broad tires and the gear struts of the aircraft need to be able to take a punch, especially on rough terrain. In normal conditions the tires need to be changed about every 25 landings, but this is cut in two when landing on unpaved or rough runways.

Photo: Andreas Zeitler

Photo: Marcus Fülber

Above: The nose landing gear of this LTG61 Transall is being retracted into the wheel bay. Notice the two gear doors, of which the forward one is always closed, except when the gear is being lowered or retracted. On the ground, the aft gear door is kept parallel with the fuselage, as can be seen in the photo to the left. The nose gear simply folds forwards into the bay, while the main gear folds upwards.

Photo: Jens Schymura

Above & right: The nose wheel landing gear strut, looking straight up. Notice the cables running over it and on the landing bay ceiling. A large hydraulically operated actuator pushed the strut forward when the landing gear is retracted. Notice the colour of the interior, which is pale green and kind of reminds me of RLM 02.

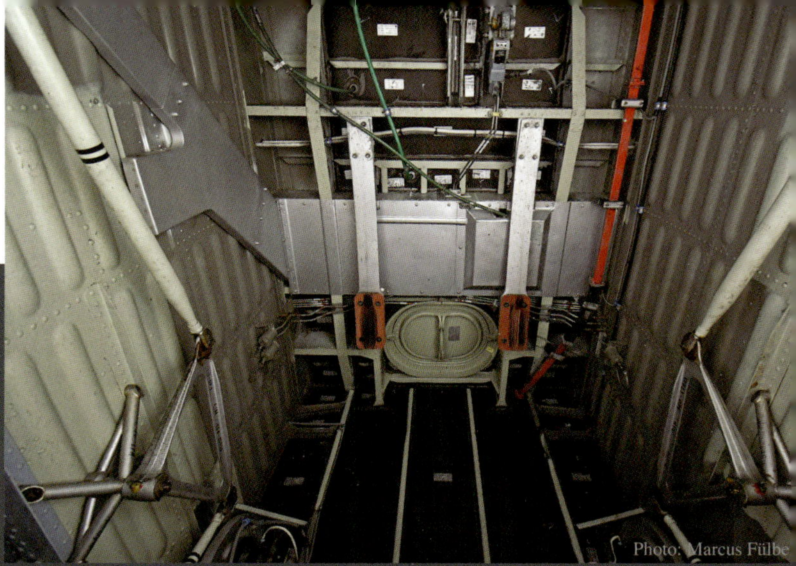

Photo: Marcus Fülbe

Above: Giving that the nose landing gear is very low to the ground, this photo needed some serious contortionism to make. This is the forward landing gear bay, looking forward. Notice the forward gear door actuators on either side of the bay.

Photo: Marcus Fülber

Transall C-160
Front Landing Gear

Photo: Marcus Fülber

Photo: Laurent Heyligen

Above: Landing the Transall, nosewheel first - now there's something that doesn't look all that comfortable... but it does show the sturdiness of the landing gear. During a "Sarajevo Approach", timing is everything... - see page 52.

Photo: Marcus Fülber

Photo: Jens Schymura

Photo: Laurent Heyligen

Photo: Marcus Fülber

Above: Making a fast turn on the grass of La Ferté Allais during the annual air show: it not only shows how strong the landing gear of the Transall is, but also how agile it can be on unpaved runways, which can come handy when operating in hostile environments. An impressive demonstration by the Armée de l'Air.

Left: A Luftwaffe Transall has been placed on jacks and has its landing gear retracted, giving a good view how it folds into the main gear bay. The main gear doors can be lifted in two parts for maintenance or when the tires need to be replaced.

Photo: Jens Schymura

Above: The main gear is equipped with two large gear doors, one on each side of the bay. The upper part of the doors are usually closed and only lifted for maintenance or checks. This Transall is taking off and because of the simple mechanics, the landing gear is up with the doors closed in a matter of seconds.

Right: Parked on the ground, this photo shows just how close the fuselage actually is to the ground: not even the height of a tire! The landing bay doors are a mere inches of the ground as well, but the upper part of the doors can be lifted in order to get access to the tires or the landing gear mechanism. Looking at these tires, just a few more landings before they need to be replaced...

Photo: Jens Schymura

Photo: Jens Schymura

Left: The starboard main landing gear of the Transall in detail. These are actually two sets of gear connected to each other to make sure that everything is lowered or lifted simultaniously. The engineers of the aircraft did everything possible to keep this system strong, simple and rugged. Have a look at the interior of the landing gear bay: hardly any lines run through it.

Right: This is a close-up of the forward part of the port main gear door. Look at the black stains coming from the APU - Auxiliary Pcwer Unit - exhaust. In this photo, the upper part of the main gear doors are lifted too. Look at the small actuator for the lower part fitted to the front of the door. The interior of the doors is painted white, while the gear struts and rims are painted light grey.

Photo: Stephan Ortmann

Right: The starboard main landing gear, looking forward. The strong landing gear is one of the most important assets of the Transall, making sure the crew can get on the ground safely, even in emergencies. This was the case in September of 2008, when Transal 50 + 50 was flying at low level in the region of Hanover and it hit the trees. Eventhough the tail and stabilisers were badly damaged, the crew was able to perform a safe emergency landing at Wunstorf AB, without any injuries. Unfrtunately, that wasn't the case for the aircraft which was beyond repair and was written off...

Photo: Jens Schymura

Below: Another look at the main landing gear door on the port side, looking aft. Look at the stains from the APU exhaust, situated immediately in front of the door.

Photo: Marcus Fülber

Photo: Jens Schymura

Above: The aft part of the starboard main landing gear in detail. Look at the fabric covered area which folds upwards during retraction. Very few lines run over the gear struts. Notice the metal bar in the background and the colour of the landing gear bay walls.

Right & below: These photos picture the port main landing gear; notice the stencilling at the front of it and the red wires running along it. In these photos the upper part of the door is lifted, which is only done during checks, tire changes or maintenance. The door is kept up by means of a strut located at the front of the gear bay. The photo below shows the gear looking aft. The black stains near the front are from the APU exhaust, which is located just in front of the port main gear.

Photo: Stephan Ortmann

Photo: Stephan Ortmann

Transall C-160
Main Landing Gear

Photo: Marcus Fülber

Photo: Stephan Ortmann

Photo: Stephan Ortmann

Above left: A close-up of the forward part of the port main gear, looking upwards; showing exactly where the red wiring goes. Look how the lower part of the gear is protected by a metal plate, preventing damage from debris coming from unpaved runways.

Above: The front part of the gear, this time looking forward.

Left: Another photo showing just how close the fuselage is to the ground. Can't be more than a few cm, right? Looks like the Good Year tire has had it's best time and will shortly need to be replaced. Noticable is the structure of the interior of the bay and the rivets running along it.

Photo: Marcus Fülber

Above: Transall 50 + 54 is taking off for another delivery of goods. Look at the extended landing gear with a total of 10 wheels.

Photo: Jens Schymura

Right: A French Transall visiting Hohn airbase. This frontal view perfectly shows how wide the main landing gear is positionned and how very low the aircraft sits on the ground. Look at the taxi light located in front of the nose landing gear, in the front landing gear door.

Transall C-160
Main Landing Gear

Photo: Laurent Heyligen

Photo: Stephan Ortmann

Above: Touchdown! A C-160D of LTG61 lands at Eindhoven air base in September of 2020, carrying a pair of chaff/Flare pods near the wing tips. Compare the camouflage of this aircraft with the one of the aircraft on the opposite page.

LTG61 was formed in 1957 and was based the airbase of Landsberg-Lech in Bavaria, in the south of Germany. When the Luftwaffe was starting to replace the Transall by the A400M Atlas, it was decided to house the new aircraft at Wunstorf and disband the Air Transport Wing 61. This occured in 2017. The remaining Transalls were handed over to LTG63. During the 60 years of LTG61, the unit flew the C-47 Dakota, Nordatlas, Dornier Do-28, UH-1D helicopter and the Transall.

Photo: Marcus Fülber

Above: This photo gives a good idea of just how high the vertical tail of the Transall actually is. The navigation light on top of the tail sits at 11,65 meters of height.
Below: A close-up of the tip of the vertical tail with the antenna at the front.

Photo: Jens Schymura

Photo: Jens Schymura

Vertical Tail

The vertical tail of the aircraft is placed high on the fuselage, making sure the area is clear when equipment is driven into the cargo bay. The large surface vertical tail has a long base running all the way up to the base of the wings. It has a large rudder, as can be seen in this photo. The leading edge of the fin is painted black and about halfway along this area, a long HF antenna is located, running all the way to the forward part of the fuselage. Notice the structure, panels and rivets, as well as the loop antenna near the top of the tail.

Photo: Stephan Ortmann

Photo: Marcus Fülber

Above: The aft end of the rudder is placed perfectly vertical as can be seen in this photo of a C-160D, carrying a logo to celebrate the 60th anniversary of the Luftwaffe. Notice the white blade antennas on the starboard wing.

Below left: The front of the base of the vertical tail.

Below: Halfway through to the base of the vertical tail, another bulge can be seen. Look at the rivets and large screws in this area.

Photo: Stephan Ortmann

Photo: Stephan Ortmann

Transall C-160
Vertical Tail

Photo: Stephan Ortmann

The high placed tail of the C-160 allows easy access to the cargo bay. And the cargo can be surprisingly large; French Transalls were used to transport helicopters, military vehicles and even Jaguar fighter jets! Like is the case today with the A400M, the transition to the Transall could take some time in France, over 50 years ago. Even though the first of the type were delivered by the end of the 1960s, the final Noratlas aircraft of 64 Squadron were replaced in 1982. By that time, its role was taken over by the newly delivered C-160NG. The unit continued to fly the Transall until 2017, when it was put on hold until September 2021, when it was reactivated on the A400M Atlas.

Above: This photo shows the vertical tail of the C-160G of the Armée de l'Air and although this version has a completely different mission, the tail fin is identical to the transport version, apart from the small electronics bulge on the side of the base. This bulge can be found on either side of the aircraft.

Photo: Jens Schymura

Photo: Andreas Zeitler

Photo: Andreas Zeitler

Above: A heavily faded grey paintjob makes this Transall of 64 Squadron, based at Evreux, look very cool. This photo shows to good effect the placement of the horizontal tails, high on the aft fuselage. At the trailing edge is a large elevator tab. As with the wings, the leading edge of the horizontal tails are painted black. Notice how near the tip of the starboard elevator, stains can be seen made by the engine exhaust.

Right: The aft fuselage and the area where the horizontal tails are fixed to it of a French Transall. Notice the lowered elevator tabs. On the central part, 4 static dischargers are located. To the right, a fuel vent can be seen. At the base of the vertical tail, a pair of Radar Warning Receivers ensure that the crew know when missiles are fires at them from behind.

Photo: Marcus Fülber

Above: The Retro Brummel of LTG63 shows off its elegant lines. I said it before, but I really like this livery. The aircraft will be missed. Look at the size of those horizontal tails!

Photo: Jens Schymura

Left: The aft fuselage and where the horizontal tail is attached to it. The area is filled with rivets to ensure a strong fuselage, which can get a heavy pounding when landing on unpaved runways. Look at the heavily weathered paintjob on this Luftwaffe Transall.

Cargo Bay

In this chapter, we show what it's all about for the Transall: the cargo bay. The photo above shows just how low the aircraft sits on the ground, allowing very easy access to the cargo bay from behind. The cargo bay has two large doors, with the lower one being the ramp and the upper one folding up to make the clearance hight as comfortable as possible. The ramp is covered with material, preventing crew and cargo from slipping and sliding.

Photo: Andreas Zeitler

Photo: Jens Schymura

Right: Standing halfway through the cargo bay, looking forward, this is what you see. Notice the ladder giving access to the emergency exit on top of the aircraft. To the left is the opening, leading either to the cockpit or to the crew exit on the left - notice the access ladder fixed onto the entry door.

Below: The right side of the cargo bay, near the front of the aircraft.

Below right: This is a closer look at the closed lateral cargo door from the inside. Notice the release handles and hinges.

Photo: Jens Schymura

Photo: Marcus Fülber

Photo: Jens Schymura

Above: This photo shows almost the entire length of the cargo bay. The entire area is pressurised in flight; look at all the padding on the side walls and ceiling. The cargo compartment is 17,20 meter long, 3,15 meter wide and just under 3 meter high. Because the aircraft's wing is actually placed on top of the fuselage, the cargo bay can be fully used.

Right: An emergency escape hatch is located in the ceiling, near the front of the cargo compartment. Whenever the aircraft has to ditch over see, this would be the exit to select. Forward of it, in the cockpit, a similar escape exit is located in the ceiling.

Photo: Marcus Füllber

Photo: Marcus Fülber

Left: This photo shows the area above the crew entrance door and the handle that is used to open it. Notice that in this area the padding is dark grey, similar to the cockpit.

Except for the Transall R, NG and G, a large lateral cargo door is located at the port forward fuselage, immediately aft of the crew entrance door. The photos below and below left show the entrance door in closed position, with immediately aft of it the cargo door. In the top corners, actuators are fixed. Look at the spot lights attached to it.

Photo: Jens Schymura

Photo: Jens Schymura

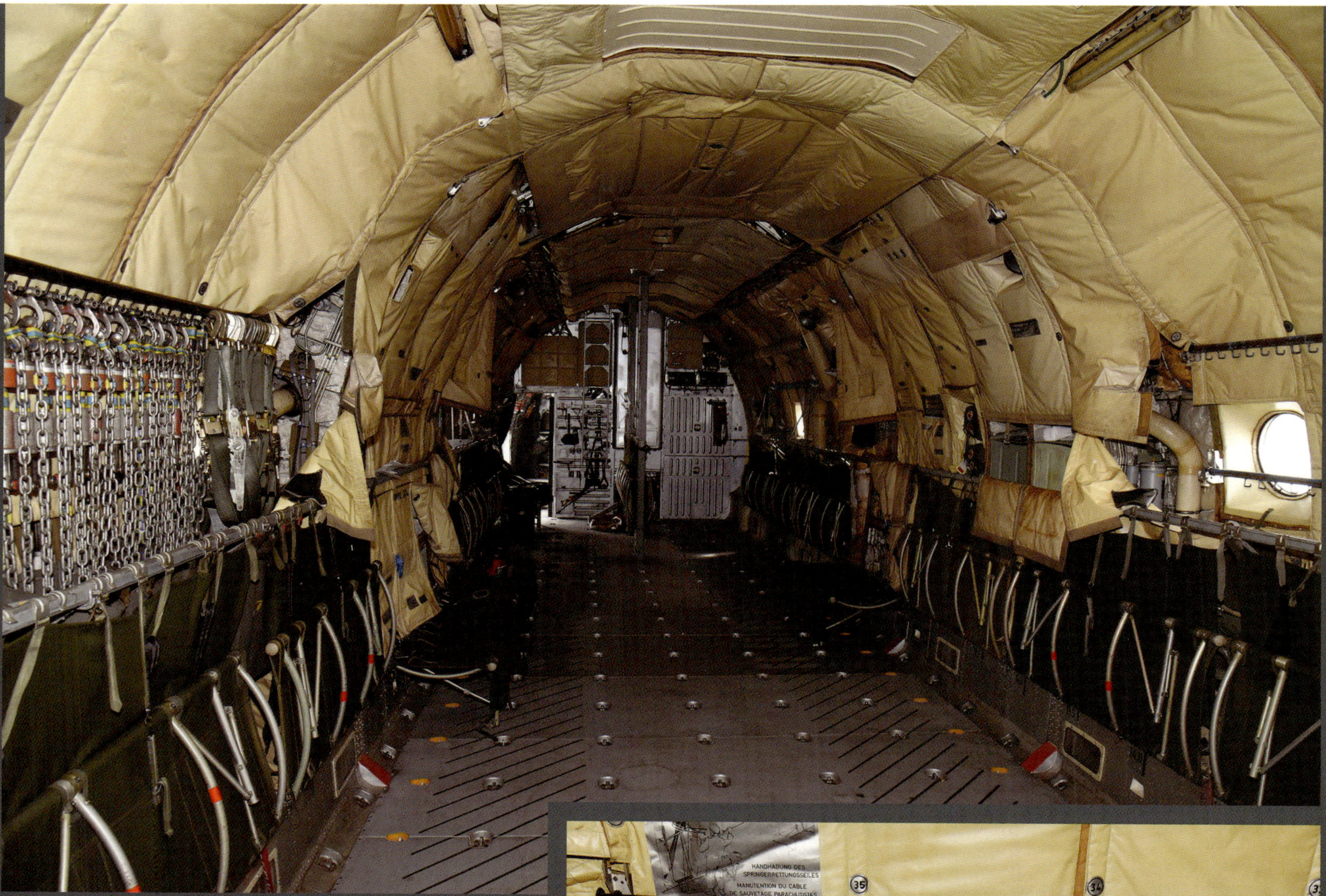

Photo: Marcus Fülber

Photo: Marcus Fülber

Above: The entire cargo bay, this time with seats for the troops attached to the side of it. Look at the cargo floor, with sandpaper-like strips fixed to it. To the left side, chains are stored which are used to fix cargo or vehicles to the floor.
The empty weight of the C-160 is 27,78 ton, while the maximum take off weight - including cargo and fuel - is an impressive 51 tons. The maximum cargo weight is 16 tons, which is about 3 ton less than the maximum capacity of the C-130H.

Photo: Marcus Fülber

Above: This is the top left hand corner of the lateral fuselage cargo door, which has, similar to the right hand corner - see page 77 - a large actuator and a spot light. Notice the black handle to the side of it, which manually operates the pump. The second batch of C-160s ordered by the Armée de l'Air didn't have the lateral doors because they were hardly ever used.

Photo: Marcus Fülber

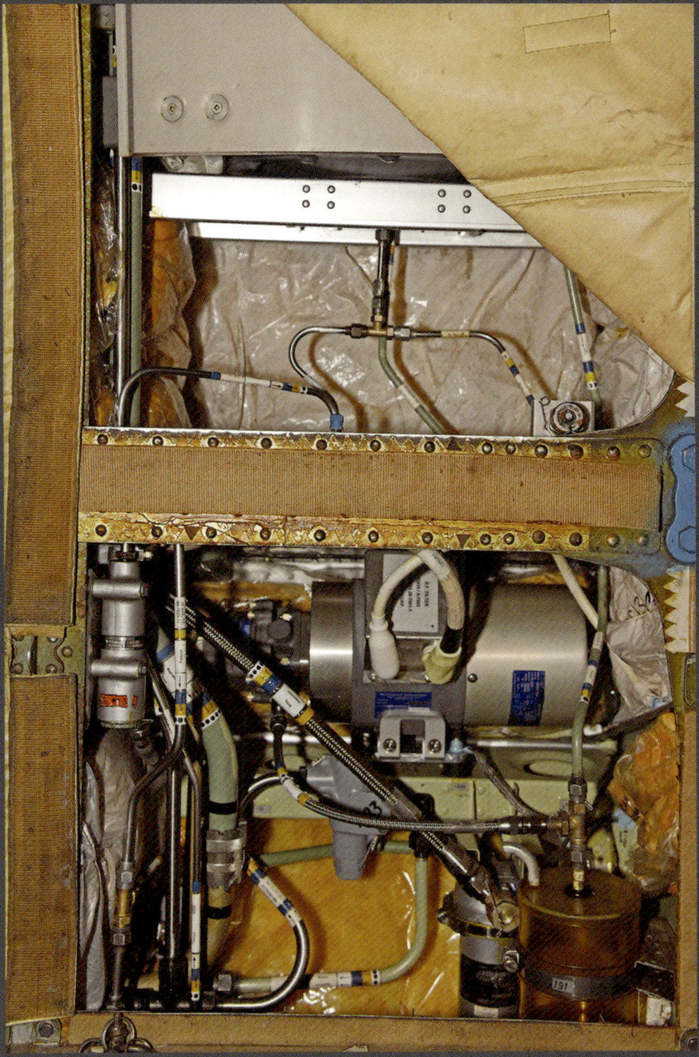

hoto: Marcus Fülber

Above and left: In the cargo bay, behind the padding, some of the aircaft's equipment can be accessed. In some areas, additional storage room is available for the crew.

Immediatly after the aircraft was introduced, the C-160 was sent on operational missions, some military, some humanitarian. After a heavy earthquake in Peru in 1970, the French government sent Transalls to the country to help the local authorities. As recent as as 2020, they were used for humanitarian missions in Gabon, in the west of central Africa.

Photo: Jens Schymura

Photo: Jens Schymura

Left: A view of the cargo bay ramp. Additional plating can be used when vehicles need to be driven into the cargo compartment. Look at the structure of the ramp and the two bars on either side of it.

Above: Standing in the cargo bay, looking to the right, this is the starboard troop door. To open it, it is pulled inwards and pushed upwards. A similar door is located on the opposite side of the fuselage. Look at the lower grey part which can be pushed horizontally and serves as a step for paratroopers. To the side, equipment storage room can be seen for medical kits, a fire extinguisher or communication equipment.

The photos on this page are a bit of a side step, but to be honest, I didn't know exactly where to put them... After entering the aircraft, it takes a few steps to get into the cockpit, however, behind the steps is an equipment bay where a lot of cables run and avionics are stowed. The photo to the right shows the four steps towards the cockpit with the pilot's seat to the left and the flight engineer's to the right. Look at the padding at the ceiling with the overhead instrument panel. Behind the co-pilot's seat is room for the navigator's station.

Photo: Marcus Fülber

Photo: Marcus Fülber

Left: Looking behind the steps, this is what you see. To the left, underneath the diagonally placed black plate, is the forward landing gear bay. Above it, the aircraft's avionics are stored. On the ceiling of this cramped areas, electrical wiring is fixed.

Photo: Jens Schymura

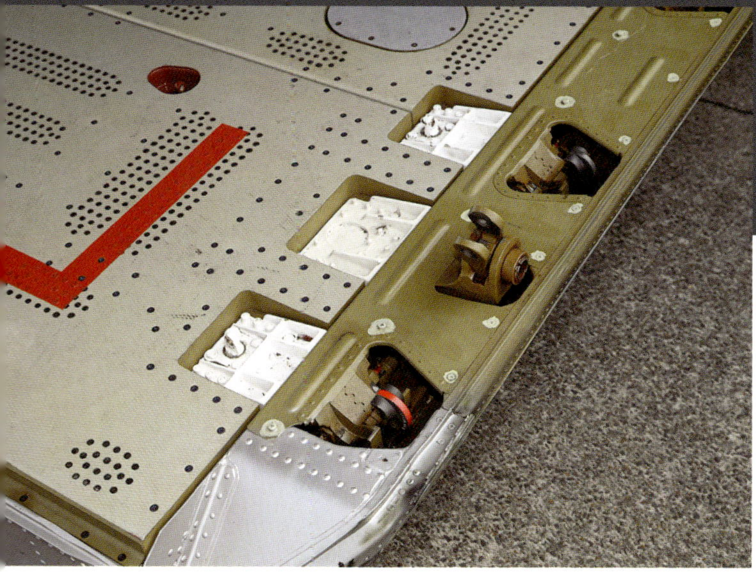

Photo: Jens Schymura

Above: On either side of the cargo bay ramp, an actuator is located. Look at the structure on the inside of the fuselage walls and the red-painted hook-up points, the reinforcements one the outside and the proximity of the troop doors.

Left: A close-up of the cargo ramp and the connection points where it fits into the upper fuselage when closed. These photos show once more just how close to the ground the Transall actually is, ensuring easy access for epuipment and vehicles, which is a true asset, especially in hard to reach areas with unpaved runway. It is one of the reasons why the Transall had such a long and successful career.

hoto: Jens Schymura

Photo: Jens Schymura

Below: This photo shows the closed cargo bay, looking aft, with at the front the cargo ramp and behind it the large cargo bay door, which folds upwards when the bay is opened. Again, notice the U-shaped fuselage reinforcements.

Photo: Jens Schymura

Above: In the ceiling of the aft part of the cargo bay, an integrated winch system is located, which helps the crew to bring heavy loads aboard the aircraft. Notice the many U-shaped bulckheads in this part of the aircraft. The photo above right, the aft part of the area can be seen. Look at the equipment and wiring fixed to the ceiling.

Photo: Jens Schymura

Maintaining the Transall

Without extensive maintenance, no aircraft flies and that is not different for the C-160 Transall. For this chapter, one of my favorite ones, we step into the maintenance hangar at Hohn airbase. These pages will show you a wealth of details, otherwise hidden by panels. These pages are dedicated to the many technicians and engineers, ensuring for more than 50 years that the aircraft remain in operational condition.

The photo to the left pictures a Transall placed on jacks in the maintenance hangar. Notice that the wheels of the forward landing gear have been removed and the opened lateral cargo bay door. Around the engines, metal racks are placed to obtain easy access.

Below: A Transall of LTG61 is undergoing maintenance as well. The radome has been lifted to get access to the weather radar. Notice the black painted interior of this area. This photo also shows the landing light in the forward landing gear door and the battery compartment aft of the radome.

Photo: Andreas Zeitler

Photo: Marcus Fülber

The aircraft's radome folds upwards and stays in place by means of a pair of struts. The photo to the left shows the aircraft during landing gear tests; which is why the forward gear door is in this position. The emergency access door on the starboard side has been removed.

Below: The Transall is equipped with a weather radar, allowing the aircraft to navigate even in bad weather conditions. The photos below show the small radar dish and its fixture to the bulckhead behind it. To ensure maximum efficiancy, the radome has to be left unpainted or, in the case of the Turkish aircraft, painted with special paint in very thin layers.

Photo: Andreas Zeitler

Photo: Marcus Fülber

Right: The radar compartment is painted black on the inside. Notice the round antenna next to the opened radome. On either side of the nose, a battery compartment is located, which can be opened by means of two quick release push buttons. The photos below show these comparments; starboard below, port below right. Look at the structure of the doors, which are held in place with two telescopic struts and the battery, which slides out by means of two simple rails.

Photo: Andreas Zeitler

Photo: Jens Schymura

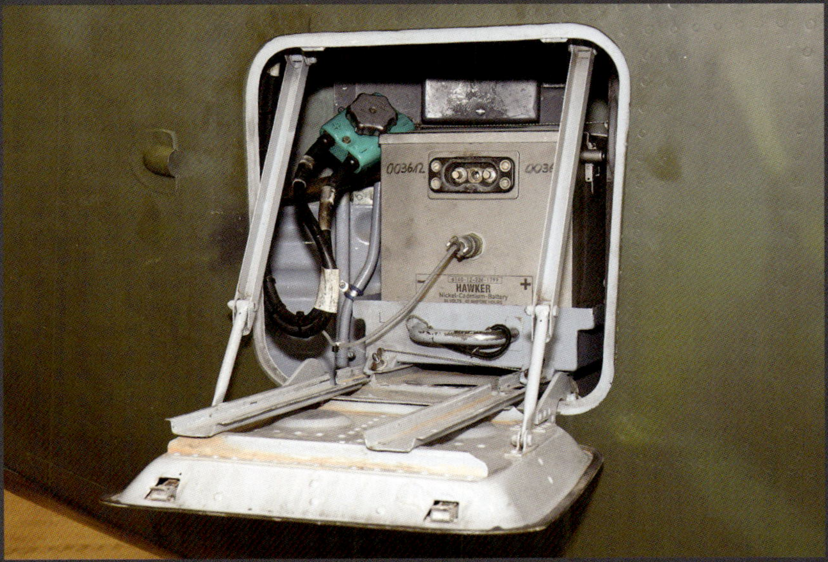

Photo: Marcus Fülber

Photo: Marcus Fülber

Photo: Marcus Fülber

Above: During a visit to the Hohn maintenance hangar, Marcus Fülber was able to take this photo, showing undercarriage retraction tests. In the forward part of the starboard landing gear sponson, the air conditionning system is located.

Above right: Aft of the air conditionning equipment, the ground refuelling point can be found. The standard Transall has 4 fuel cells, however the French Transall NG, R and G have a fifth fuel bay on top of the cargo bay, in the base of the wing.

Right: Inspection work is being carried out on this Transall. Notice the trailing edge flaps are removed and checks are being done on the landing light located in the wing's leading edge.

Photo: Marcus Fülber

Photo: Marcus Fülber

In the forward part of the port main landing gear sponson, the aircraft APU - Auxiliary Power Unit - is located. This system ensures the delivery of compressed air for the main engine start, but also provides power for the air conditioning and the heating systems of the aircraft. The cut-out photos show the APU removed from the aircraft. The photo below shows the right side of the APU, above right is the left part of it, which is visible when the access door is open.

Photo: Jens Schymura

Photo: Marcus Fülber

Photo: Marcus Fülber

Above: The port engine of this Transall is being checked on the tarmac of Hohn airbase. The starboard engine door has been folded - if you look closely, you'll see that the lower engine door is fixed to it. Ground power is taken from the cart to the left of the aircraft.

Photo: Marcus Fülber

Right: A spare Rolls-Royce RTy.20 Tyne Mk 22 turboprop engine, sitting in its container. Behind it is another one. Although the engine is capable of providing 6,100 hp, it does have its limitations, as was noticed when flying at high altitudes, such as over the mountains in Afghanistan.

Right: Look at all the details in this photo of the port engine. There are 4 doors around the forward part of the engine, with the lower door connected to the starboard one and the upper door to the port one. Look at the actuator connected to the engine strut and the structure on the inside of the doors and the fasteners on the edges of them. Notice that the propellers are in feathered position.
The air intake on the lower door can be seen from the inside in this photo.
On the side of the engine near the lower orange tube, you can see where exhausts and filters connect to the inner parts of the engine doors.

Photo: Marcus Fülber

Below: When electrical power is needed during check on the tarmac, this is provided by a cart such as this one. The hook-up is located at the front of the port main landing gear sponson.

Photo: Marcus Fülber

Photo: Jens Schymura

Photo: Jens Schymura

Photo: Jens Schymura

Some really close-up photos of the Rolls-Royce RTy.20 Tyne Mk 22 turboprop engine. The photo top left shows the actuator of the port engine door - see how the top engine panel is fixed to it? The photo above shows the electrical wiring running in a metal rail over the engine.

The photo to the left pictures the inside of the starboard engine door, seen from the front with the lower door attached to it. Notice the exhaust duct on it and the air intake duct in the lower door. The interior is metal, with the edges painted in light olive green.

Photo: Marcus Fülber

Photo: Marcus Fülber

Photo: Jens Schymura

Photo: Marcus Fülber

Rolls-Royce RTy.20 Tyne Mk 22

These photos show the starboard engine of the Transall. The engine, which was originally designed for the Vickers Vanguard, an airliner that can hardly be described as a success with only 44 ever built, is a twin-spool turboprop with a legnth of 2,76 meter. The light grey area behind the black ring at the front houses the oil system of the engine, which lubricates all engine components and supplies oil for the propeller hydraulic operation. The part underneath the main engine is the starter system, with a high pressure fuel pump which supplies fuel to the burners.

Photo: Marcus Fülb

Transall C-160 Engine

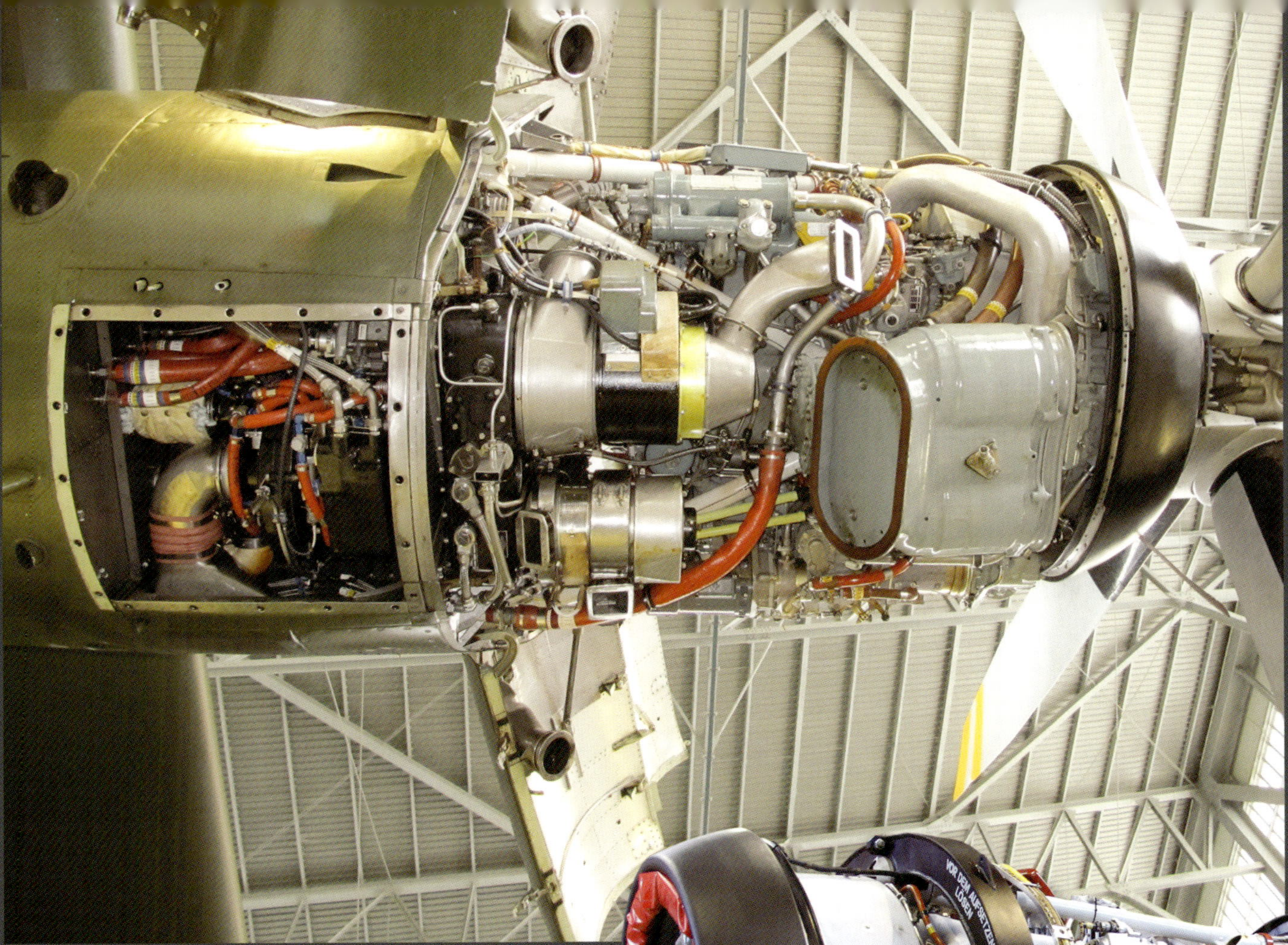

Photo: Marcus Fülber

Left: Looking up at the starboard engine. Near the front is the fuel system.

Below: the Tyne engine on its dolly. To the side of the port side of the engine, the water/ methanol system is located, which determines the flow and RPM when dicharge commences. Below it is the engine control system.

Photo: Marcus Fülber

Above: a close-up of the entire starboard engine panel with the cables and drains running over it. it is fixed to the engine by means of two hinges and opened by a single actuator. Look at the engine fixtures to the right, painted in white, on which the engine itself is mounted.

Photo: Marcus Fülber

Right: engine panels can be opened individually, as this photo shows. With the lower engine door removed, maintenance crew can check the air intake filter and the fuel system located underneath the engine's compressor. Both these parts of the engine can be seen in detail in the two photos below.

The engine has an axial compressor with 6 low pressure stages and 9 high pressure stages. In this type of engine, the air flows parallel to the axis of rotation. Each stage has a row of rotating blades that accelerate the air coming from the intake. The aft located combustors and turbine will then provide the aircraft with the necessary thrust.

Photo: Marcus Fülber

Photo: Marcus Fülber

Photo: Jens Schymura

Above: The engine, looking up from the ground, seen from front to back the photo next to it shows the same area, this time looking forward. The turbine inlet temperature of the Rolls-Royce RTy.20 Tyne Mk 22 engine is 800 °C.
The engine is equipped with a fuel drainage system, allowing the risk of burning fuel in case of an engine fire. In such a case, any unburnt fuel is collected and vented.

Some characteristics of the Tyne engine: it has a dry weight of 1,085 kg and a compressor ration of 13.5:1 - with this the design power and specific fuel consumption are obtained. Information coming from the engine is indicated on many instruments in the cockpit, to ensure optimal functioning: the turbine gas temperature, torque, low pressure and high pressure RPM, vibration, fuel and oil flow, etc.

Photo: Jens Schymura

Photo: Marcus Fülber

Photo: Marcus Fülber

When operating in hostile environments, upgraded Transalls are equipped with several defence systems. These consist of Radar Warning Receivers on the nose and the base of the vertical base. In addition to these, chaff and flares can be fired to divert incoming missiles; flares for infra-red missiles and chaff for missiles equipped with a radar guiding system. The photo above shows a Luftwaffe Transall firing flares during a demonstration flight.

Photo: Jens Schymura

Photo: Marcus Fülber

Photo: Jens Schymura

Chaff and flare dispencers are located aft on the port main gear sponson, or are bolted on the top of the fuselage. German aircraft can be equipped with two under-wing Modular Countermeasure Pods, MCP-10, each containing ten magazines. These pods are placed near the wing tips, always dropping the flares downwards and outwards.

Right: Look at the details of the wing pylon to which the Modular Countermeasure Pods are fixed. You see the ten stations each containing room for 30 cartridges?

Photo: Malaury Buis, Armée de l'Air et de l'Espace

Taking care of business

The action chapter of the Transall book! The one thing that is typical for the C-160 is that it did a great job for decades in all discretion. Being a trusted workhorse, it transported thousands of tons all around the world, making sure that both military personnel and civilians got the goods whenever and where ever they were needed.

The photo below shows the C-160D in its farewell livery. 2021 signaled the final year of operations for the German Transall and for the occasion, this high-viz paintjob was presented. The photo to the left shows one of the few C-160G Gabriels in flight over the industrial port of Dunkirk in 2019. Look at the lowered radome on the belly of the aircraft. Notice at all those antennas all around te fuselage and the fuselage pod aft of the troop door. See the long fins underneath the landing gear sponsons and the air intake for the equipment at the end of it. A unique feature for the C-160G. So, strap in for a couple of pages of the Transall in action!

Photo: Marcus Fülber

Photo: Marcus Fülber

Two more photos of the last of the German Transalls to receive a special livery: the Retro Brummel on its Goodbye Tour. Look at the stylised 63 on the port aft fuselage. The dayglo on the outboard of the engines, rudder and forward part of the main gear sponsons give it a very cool and indeed retro look!

Photo: Andreas Zeitler

Photo: Marcus Fülber

Photo: Andreas Zeitler

Above: This Transall has clearly seen better days. 50 + 53 has some panels missing on the vertical tail and underneath the wings and when it comes to patchwork, this one goes through to the finals at the Olympics. Birds seem to love it though!

Left: A heavily weathered Luftwaffe Transall is dropping flares. See where the cartridges are coming from?

Photo: Peter Anthoni

Above: A heavily weathered Transall is turning onto the active runway and is moment away from getting underway to its next mission. Notice the position of the trailing edge flaps. Once the aircraft is airborn and at altitude, the throttles need to be at 40 degrees or less. 40 degrees is the in flight idle position.

Photo: Andreas Zeitler

Right: Here's an odd one from the Luftwaffe - this Transall comes back from a visit to the maintenance shop after a big overhaul and is ready for a test flight. The paint has been stripped from the fuselage to the bare metal. Look at the colours of the base of the vertical tail, the rudder and the port wing leading edge as well as the vapor coming from the tips of the propellors.

Photo: Andreas Zeitler

Photo: Andreas Zeitler

Above, right: These two photos show Else, the Transall of LTG63 that made the last flight to Kunduz in Afghanistan in 2013. Notice the zappings around the crew entrance door and the very weary finish of the camouflage.

Below: The Turkish demonstration team "Turkish Stars", flying the F-5E Tiger II, have this special painted Transall as a support aircraft.

Photo: Jens Schymura

Photo: Laurent Heyligen

Above: Landing on a grass airstrip, that isn't a problem for the Transall. Might be if you are sensitive to hay fever though... Notice the deployed speedbrakes.

Photo: Peter Anthoni

Right: The French Transalls can also be used as an aerial refuelling aircraft, for which a refuelling hose is located in the port main gear sponson. In this photo, the hose has been extended and a Mirage 2000 is closing in for some much needed fuel. This photo also gives you a good idea of the size of the C-160!

Photo: Jean-Luc Brunet, Armée de l'Air et de l'Espace

Above: A C-160 Gabriel on patrol over the Atlantic Ocean. Look at the different antennas in the starboard and port wing tip electronics pods. The two aircraft operating in this configuration continue to fly until 2025, when they will be replaced by Dassault Falcons in the same role.

Photo: Peter Anthoni

Right: A C-160R equipped with an in-flight refuelling system is making a hard turn to the right with the refuelling hose extended. Notice the orange lines painted underneath the port main gear sponson, helping pilots to line up with the aircraft. Look how the exhaust stains the horizontal tails and the trailing edge wing flaps.

Above: During a capability demonstration by the Luftwaffe, the take off of this Transall is covered by a Tiger attack helicopter flying along side while topcover is being given by a pair of Eurofighter Typhoons. During such demonstration, the capacity of the Transall to land and take off in a very short distance is apparent.

Right: An all grey Luftwaffe Transall? What is this witchcraft you are talking about? And look at that strange registration L + LX! Well, this aircraft was used as an instructural airframe for technicians and crew at Hohn air base and the registration is in Roman numbers, so it actually is 50 + 60. So, you could say it's quite a unique Transall!

Photo: Jens Schymura

Right: 2007 and Lufttransportgeschwader 61 is celebrating its 50th anniversary and for the occasion, painted one of their aircraft in this pop-art style livery. On the vertical tail, "Für den Frieden" is written - For Peace. LTG61 would be disbanded 10 years later, in December of 2017.

Photo: Marcus Fülber

Photo: Kris Christiaens

Left: To celebrate the 60th anniversary of the Luftwaffe's LTG61, a Transall was painted in a striking silver livery. On the tail is a detail of the unit's emblem, a mountain goat painted in black, while on the side, a roundel depicts the different aircraft with which the unit flew in the 60 years of operations: the C-47 Dakota, Transall, Noratlas N 2501 and the Bell UH-1D.

Photo: Andreas Zeitler

Above: After a Luftwaffe Transall dropped of a full load of flares, the engine wash makes the smoke coming from them twirl in the air.

Right: A close-up of a Manching-based Transall makes you almost hear the typical sound of the engines. The pilot has just lifted the landing gear lever on the central instrument panel - notice the nose gear and main gear doors about to close and the flaps about to be lifted.

Photo: Andreas Zeitler

Right: This C-160F is about to land and has the trailing edge flaps completely lowered. Notice how the wing tips are bent upwards during the manoeuvre. Notice the white blade antennas on the foward fuselage and starboard wing tip.

Below: This patchwork C-160R of the Armée de l'Air made an impressive display at the 2019 La Ferté Allais airshow, performing some very tight turns and touch-and-go manoeuvres. In this photo, the trailing edge flaps are down and the aircraft is ready to land. Notice the photo identification roundel on the main gear sponson and the landing lights in the wing's leading edge..

Photo: Peter Anthoni

Photo: Andreas Zeitler

Photo: Kris Christiaens

Left: An all white Luftwaffe C-160 Transall is about to take off from RAF Fairford, after another edition of the International Air Tattoo. Look at the underside panel of the wing's leading edge, which is painted grey. Being white, it shows to good effect where the aircraft weathers the most, like aft of the APU in the main gear sponson.

Photo: Peter Anthoni

Above: A pair of smart-looking ghost grey painted Turkish Transalls. Notice that these aircraft don't have the lateral cargo door on the port side of the fuselage. Notice the black painted leading edges of the wings, vertical and horizontal tails and the red-and-white painted propellor tips.

Photo: Marcus Fülber

Duke Hawkins

When going over my bookshelves, some aircraft seem to be left aside by some editors. It is true that some aircraft are more spectacular than others, but still, many of the more unknown aircraft also deserve their spot in aviation history. And being driven on passion more than good business instinct, we wanted to include the C-160. The C-160 Transall has been doing his job discretely for many decades, airlifting thousands of men and tons of equipment all around the world. This agile, twin-engined transport aircraft has been the backbone for the German, French, Turkish and South African Air Forces and when you look at it more closely, is truly an amazing aircraft. In this book, we bring you a complete portrait of the C-160 Transall, not only in its role as a transport aircraft, but also as the electronic warfare variant C-160G, referred to as "Gabriel". Most of the photos in this book were taken by Jens Schymura and Marcus Fülber in Hohn airbase. So, we not only want to thank both of them, but also the commander and people of the base. For some of the photos of the Gabriel were obtained with the help of Julien Fechter of Sirpa Air.

I hope you like the result and thank you for purchasing this book. If you got it from a friend, thanks him or her from us for a good choice! We're already working on the next one, but if you have suggestions, don't hesitate to let us know, our website is on the back cover!

Duke